MORNING & EVENING
—— *with the* ——
SPIRITUAL
CLASSICS
40 Days of Meditations

*Compiled and Prepared for the
Modern Reader by Bernard Bangley*

HAROLD
SHAW
PUBLISHERS

Wheaton, Illinois

ISBN 0-87788-534-6

Edited by Lil Copan and Cindy Crosby
Cover photo © 1999 by Luci Shaw

05 04 03 02 01 00 99

10 9 8 7 6 5 4 3 2 1

Printed in Colombia

Introduction

You are holding a unique devotional guide. It makes the most respected spiritual writing of many centuries available for easy reading and meditation. These works have a particular devotional value for our present day. The contemporary importance of these "classics" continually amazes me.

Many of the writers included in these readings are famous. Their books will always be in print and widely available. Others are obscure. You will understand why a dedicated few have preserved the writings of all these spiritual authors once you have tasted the little samples in this book. It is my hope that you will be motivated to read some of these writers in their original, complete works.

Many of these writers are also held captive by the writing style of their era. They look stuffy and cold on paper. What I have done is to paraphrase their writings into clear, simple, modern English. I wanted to make them accessible to people who might get bogged down struggling with the original versions. I have shortened sentences and expressed their ideas with dignified but commonplace language.

Although I have expressed their thoughts and statements in modern English, I have not put any words into their mouths. While freely paraphrasing for quick reading, I have resisted every temptation to introduce new elements. They aren't needed. These pages were lively when they were first written and remain lively today.

There are many ways to use a book like this. Maybe for you it will provide a daily moment of quiet devotion in a busy life. A blessed moment it will be! Prepare yourself for the fact that you may not be able to escape the implications of what you have read for the remainder of that day.

On the other hand, one page might lead to another. You may find it hard to put down. This is beneficial too. Although these pages are not intended for continuous reading, it may be that you can read until you come to the one that speaks to your present circumstance. Then you can slow down and meditate upon what God is saying to you.

Above all, read prayerfully. God can speak through these writers. Go ahead and give God an opportunity with your soul. Be still and listen. Good things will come of it.

—Bernard Bangley

Day 1—Morning

Getting Started

As the deer pants for streams of water, so my soul pants for you, O God. *Psalm 42:1*

Our soul is like a castle created out of a precious jewel. There are many interesting rooms in this beautiful castle of the soul.

How do we enter? Is that a foolish question? After all, if the castle is your own soul you are already rather intimate with it! What you must realize is that there are many different ways we can exist within this castle. You can remain with the guards in the courtyard outside the gate. You can live your entire life and never discover what it's like inside.

The doorway into the castle is genuine prayer and meditation. Mechanical repetitions of prayers are insufficient. They will leave you like the paralytic who waited beside the pool of Bethesda: He stayed there helplessly for thirty-eight years until the Lord himself came along to help him.

—Teresa of Avila: *Interior Castle*

Day 1—Evening

Walking with God

I stay close to you; your right hand upholds me.
Psalm 63:8

There is nothing in the world as delightful as a continual walk with God. Only those who have experienced it can comprehend it. And yet I do not recommend that you seek it solely because it is so enjoyable. Do it because of love, and because it is what God wants. If I were a preacher, the one thing I would preach about more than anything else is the practice of the presence of God.

Please get started now. I don't care how old you are. It is better late than never.

I can't imagine how any faithful person can be satisfied without the practice of the presence of God. For my part, I spend as much time as possible alone with him at the very center of my soul. As long as I am with him I am afraid of nothing, but the least turning away from him is unbearable.

It is necessary to trust God completely. The various forms of devotion, as good as they are, merely help us on our way to God. But when we are already *with* God, they are of little use.

Don't be discouraged if you find this hard to do. If you just try it a little, you will consider it wasted time. Stick to it! Resolve to persevere in it until the day you die—no matter what!

—Brother Lawrence:
The Practice of the Presence of God

The World Is a Biased Judge

If the world hates you, keep in mind that it hated me first. *John 15:18*

Once it becomes evident that you intend to live a devout life, secular people will laugh at you and criticize you. The worst of them will say that because of some hard experiences you have run to God as an escape. Your friends will warn you of the unhappy consequences of your choice, saying that you will lose your reputation, become difficult to work with, or age prematurely. They will tell you that if you are going to live in the world, you must be a part of the world. They will call you an extremist and urge moderation upon you.

These foolish babblers are not concerned about you. "If you belonged to the world, it would love you as its own. As it is, you do not belong to the world, but I have chosen you out of the world. That is why the world hates you" (John 15:19).

Let some throw away many nights playing chess or cards and no one says anything about it. But if we give an hour to meditation they are ready to go for the doctor to cure us of our illness. The world is a biased judge, approving its own and dealing harshly with the children of God.

While light is a good thing, it can blind us after we have been in the dark. The change in your style of life may create some problems. Be patient. The strangeness will eventually wear off.

—Francis de Sales: *The Devout Life*

Day 2—Evening

Asking for the Right Things

Take this cup from me. Yet not what I will, but what you will. *Mark 14:36*

It is a mistake to ask God to give you what you want. Your desires are probably not in complete harmony with God's will. Pray instead that God will lead you to want the right things. Ask for what is good and for what is best for your soul. There is no way you could want these things for yourself more than God desires you to have them.

Often when I prayed, I kept asking for things that seemed good to me. I pressured God to give me what I wanted. I did not trust God enough to allow him to provide what would be best for me. When I actually received the thing I had unreasonably sought I would be embarrassed by my own selfish stubbornness. Ultimately, the thing would not turn out to be what I had expected.

Relax your prayers. Do not work so hard to have your request granted. The Lord wants to give you more than you ask. Nothing can be greater than intimate conversation with God, than being absolutely preoccupied with his companionship. Prayer that is not distracted with a wish list is the highest achievement of the intellect.

If you would ask God for something, ask to be cleansed of your passions. Pray to be delivered from ignorance. Plead with God to free you from temptation.

In your prayers, desire justice, virtue, and spiritual knowledge. The other things will be given you as well.

If you will pray for others, you will pray like the angels.

—Evagrius Ponticus: *Chapters on Prayer*

Day 3—Morning

The Value of Suffering

Our light and momentary troubles are achieving for
us an eternal glory that far outweighs them all.
2 Corinthians 4:17

It is hard to believe that a loving God could allow
us to suffer. Does it please him? Couldn't he make
us good without making us miserable? Certainly
he could. God can do anything. Our hearts are in
his hands.

But he does not choose to spare us sorrow. In
the same way that we are not born mature, but
have to grow into adulthood, so we must learn to
be humble and to trust God. We need our crosses.
Suffering can help us loosen some knots that tie
us to earth. To resist is merely to delay what God
is trying to do for us.

God works in the heart the same way he works
on the body—slowly, imperceptibly. Physical de-
velopment is steady and deliberate. Our heavenly
Father sends a series of events that wean us from
earth by gradual steps. Learning to deny ourselves
is a painful process. But the sick soul must take
its medicine. Is the surgeon cruel when he makes
an incision? No! It is an act of kindness.

The parental heart of God has no desire to hurt
us. But he understands that we must get our
priorities straight. We cry. We pout. We sigh and
groan. We say unkind things about God. He does
not intervene. He lets us continue through the
process. And we are saved. A little grief has spared
us a much greater sorrow. We can only conclude
that God is good, that he is tender and compas-
sionate even when we feel that we have a right to
complain that he is unkind.

—François de Fénelon: *Meditations and Devotions*

Day 3—Evening

A Variety of Crosses

So even though Jesus was God's Son, he learned obedience from the things he suffered. *Hebrews 5:8, NLT*

God is a clever designer of crosses. Some are as heavy as iron or lead. Others are as light as straw. He constructs impressive crosses of gold and jewels. He uses all the things we like best. In spite of their great variety, crosses have two things in common. They are hard to carry and they crucify.

A poor, hungry person bears a leaden cross. But God can bring suffering just as unpleasant to the wealthy. The poor can at least beg for a handout! The well-to-do have nowhere to turn. If poor health can be added to the glittering cross, the crucifixion is complete. Then we see both our frailty and the worthlessness of our wealth. The things that impress those looking on from the outside are invisible to the ones who possess them. One may be crucified while the world envies his good fortune! Prestige can be more painful than arthritis.

—François de Fénelon: *Meditations and Devotions*

Day 4—Morning

Reconciliation

For if, when we were God's enemies, we were reconciled to him through the death of his Son, how much more, having been reconciled, shall we be saved through his life! *Romans 5:10*

When two goats meet on a narrow bridge over deep water, what do they do? The bridge is so narrow they can neither turn around nor pass each other. If they fight they may fall into the water and be drowned.

They resolve the problem quite naturally. One lies down and the other passes over. Neither is injured.

People can learn a similar tactic. It is better to yield a little than to fall into raucous discord with others. We turn too quickly to lawyers. When people desire to be reconciled to and to reach an agreement, someone must yield, giving way to another.

This is the way we were reconciled to God. God waived his rights and controlled his wrath. Christ mediated an agreement between us. Like all peacemakers, he suffered pain. The one who separates two fighters receives the most blows. For Christ, reconciliation led to the Cross where he died for us.

—Martin Luther: *Table Talk*

Day 4 —Evening

Remarkable Love

Now the betrayer had arranged a signal with them: "The one I kiss is the man; arrest him." Going at once to Jesus, Judas said, "Greetings, Rabbi!" and kissed him. Jesus replied, "Friend, do what you came for." *Matthew 26:48-50*

Ponder how Christ loved Judas, who was his deadly enemy. Christ was good to him. He was courteous to one he knew to be damnable. He chose him as an apostle. He sent him to preach with the others. He gave him power to work miracles. He showed him the same good cheer in word and deed that he gave the other apostles.

He washed his feet and sat down at table with him. He did not speak sharply to him in front of others. He never said an evil word about him. When Judas betrayed him with a kiss, Jesus called him his friend. In all of this, Christ did not pretend or flatter. He showed honest love. Judas was not worthy of it. He deserved not even a token of love.

This kind of unconditional love is also required of us. Jesus said, "A new command I give you: Love one another. As I have loved you, so you must love one another" (John 13:34).

You protest. How can you love a bad person the same way you love a good one? Here is my answer. We are to love both, but not for the same reason. If you can love yourself only because you know you belong to God, you can love others the same way. If they are good and virtuous, you can love God who is in them. If they are bad and immoral, you can still love them—not as they are—but for the sake of God who can make them better.

—Walter Hilton: *The Scale of Perfection*

Day 5—Morning

About Prayer

Very early in the morning, while it was still dark, Jesus got up, left the house and went off to a solitary place, where he prayed. *Mark 1:35*

The proper thing is for us always to think of God and pray without ceasing. If we are not able to achieve this, we can at least set special times for prayer each day. At these designated moments we can focus entirely on God.

Here are some natural opportunities:

- when we wake in the morning
- before we begin our work
- before and after meals
- when we go to bed

This is only a start, of course. We should not think of these times of prayer as a ritual. Neither do they mean we are freed from prayer at other hours of the day. Think of these moments as nothing more than a discipline for your spiritual weakness. It is a stimulation for your groggy soul. There will be times when you are under stress, times when you will be aware of others in difficulty. Immediately turn to God in prayer. Offer prayers of thanks all through the day.

When you pray, do not put any limits on God. It is not your business to tell God how to answer your prayers. This is not a time to bargain or to set conditions. Before you tell God what you want or need, ask that his will may be done. This makes your will subordinate to his.

—John Calvin: *Of Prayer*

Tiny Prayers

"Well done, my good servant!" his master replied. "Because you have been trustworthy in a very small matter, take charge of ten cities." *Luke 19:17*

Make frequent, short little prayers to God. Express your appreciation for his beauty. Ask him to help you. Fall at the foot of the cross. Love his goodness. Give your soul to him a thousand times a day. Stretch out your hand to him like a child. If such prayerful, intimate thoughts become habitual, you will gain a beautiful familiarity with God. When you really love God, you won't be able to stop thinking about him.

On one very clear night a devout person stood by a brook watching the sky. The stars were reflected in the water. That person said, "O my God, in the same way the stars of heaven are reflected here on earth, so are we on earth reflected in heaven." Saint Francis knelt in prayer beside such a beautiful brook and became enraptured. "God's grace flows as gently and sweetly as this little stream." Another saint watched a mother hen gather little chickens under her. He said, "Lord, keep us all under the shadow of your wings."

Many little prayers like this can make up for the lack of all other prayers. They are essential. Without them rest is mere idleness and labor is pure drudgery.

—Francis de Sales: *The Devout Life*

My enemies are not the ones who sneer and make
fun. I could put up with that or even hide from them.
But it was my closest friend, the one I trusted most.
Psalm 55:12-13, CEV

Friends can hurt us more than enemies. Sometimes the very person we are trying to help turns
against us. In such a time, hear what the Lord is
saying: "Don't be sad. I have permitted this for
the benefit of your soul. I enjoy your companionship. A frightened child returns to its mother's
arms. You will find the kind of absolute faithful-
ness in me that you will not be able to find in
another person."

Let the Lord lift you to his breast as though
you were a little child. Let him hug you and soothe
you with divine kisses. He will take whatever has
been troubling you and weave it into a necklace
of bright flowers.

Then you will think of others who have greater
problems than yours. You will be bothered by
your own impatience. When the Lord assures you
of his tender love for you, placing the lightweight
necklace of brilliant flowers around your neck,
you will be strengthened. You will praise God
with much devotion.

Being able to praise God when you are troubled is a special gift.

—Gertrude of Helfta: *The Herald of Divine Love*

Day 6—Evening

Obedience to God

"I am the Lord's servant," Mary answered. "May it be to me as you have said." *Luke 1:38*

God speaks to us today in the same way that he spoke to our ancestors. In ancient times people found it natural and important to seek God's will. With little spiritual guidance, and in utter simplicity, they heard from God. There was nothing complicated about it. They understood that every moment of every day presented an opportunity for faith to fulfill a responsibility to God. They moved through the day like the hand of a clock. Minute after minute they were consciously and unconsciously guided by God.

Mary's response to the angel who announced the conception of Jesus is an example of this kind of behavior. She was a young and simple person. She completely surrendered herself to God. Her brief answer completely subjugated herself to God's intention.

Her son expressed the identical sentiment when he prayed in the Garden of Gethsemane, "My Father, if it is possible, may this cup be taken from me. Yet not as I will, but as you will" (Matthew 26:39). He teaches us to pray the same thing in the Lord's Prayer: "Thy will be done" (Matthew 6:10, KJV).

—Jean-Pierre de Caussade:
Abandonment to Divine Providence

Day 7—Morning

Moodswing

Being in anguish, he prayed more earnestly. *Luke 22:44*

So you feel one way today! You will feel another way tomorrow. Like it or not, you will be somewhat manic-depressive as long as you live.

> Some days you will be happy and other
>   days you will be sad,
> some days calm and other days troubled,
> some days faithful and other days faithless,
> some days vigorous and other days sluggish,
> some days solemn and other days
>   lighthearted.

But if you are well taught by the Spirit, you will live above such changes. You will pass through your various moods unshaken and push on toward your goal of seeking God only.

The clearer your target, the better you will weather emotional storms.

—Thomas á Kempis: *The Imitation of Christ*

You are my friends if you do what I command. *John 15:14*

Life without Jesus is like a dry garden baking in the sun. It is foolish to want anything that conflicts with Jesus. What can the world give you without Jesus? His absence is hell; his presence, paradise. If Jesus is with you, no enemy can injure you. Whoever finds Jesus has discovered a great treasure. He is the best of all possible good. The loss of him is a tremendous misfortune. Living without Jesus is poverty.

If we want to live intimately with Jesus, we will need to develop our skills. Be humble and peaceable, and Jesus will be with you. Be devout and quiet, and Jesus will reside with you.

Make many friends. Love them dearly. But love Jesus in a special way. Love others because of Jesus. Love Jesus for himself. For him, and in him, love both your friends and your enemies. Pray for them all, asking God to lead them to know and love Jesus also. Never seek this kind of devoted love for yourself. Such devotion belongs to God alone.

If discouraging and unpleasant days come your way, don't be despondent or defeated. Stand strong in God and bear whatever you must to the glory of Jesus Christ. For after winter, summer comes. After night, day returns. After a storm, calm is restored.

—Thomas á Kempis: *The Imitation of Christ*

Day 8—Morning

Imperfect Perception

Now we see but a poor reflection as in a mirror; then we shall see face to face. Now I know in part; then I shall know fully. *1 Corinthians 13:12*

Lift your heart up to God with simple love. Let God be your aim rather than the things he can provide. Try to forget the world and everything material. Focus on God alone.

When you begin you will only find darkness. This is like a cloud of unknowing. You will not be able to identify it. As you reach out to God, this dark cloud will always be between you and God. There is nothing you can do about it. It will prevent you from seeing him clearly. Neither the reasoning powers of your rational mind nor the affections of your emotions will permit a complete experience of God.

Accept this as natural. Try to be comfortable and content in this darkness for as long as it takes. Continue to call out for God. If you are going to have any kind of experience with God in this life, it will be in this cloud and in this darkness.

You have a knowing power and a loving power. God, who gave both of them to you, is incomprehensible to the knowing power. But he is entirely comprehensible to the loving power. This is the miracle of love.

Some think they ought to be able to achieve a perception of God by thinking about him. Racking your brain with intellectual effort is useless. You will misguide yourself.

—Anonymous: *The Cloud of Unknowing*

Day 8—Evening

Keep On Praying

Be joyful in hope, patient in affliction, faithful in prayer. *Romans 12:12*

With a proper attitude toward God it will be easy to learn to persevere in prayer. We will discover ways to hold our own desires in check and wait patiently for the Lord. We can be sure he is always with us. We can be confident he actually hears our prayers even when the only immediate response is silence.

It is a mistake to be like impatient children who need instant gratification. There are times when God does not respond as quickly as we would like. This is not a time to be despondent. It does not mean that God is angry with you or indifferent toward you. This is certainly not the time to give up praying. Instead of being discouraged, keep on praying.

This perseverance in prayer is highly recommended to us in the Scripture. In Psalms we read how David and others became almost weary of praying. They complained that God was not responding to their prayers. But they understood that persistent faith was a requirement, and they continued to pray.

—John Calvin: *Of Prayer*

Grab It and Growl

Some of the Lord's followers think one day is more important than another. Others think all days are the same. But each of you should make up your own mind. *Romans 14:5*, CEV

People will claim a piece of the world and think they have discovered a treasure. Then they will see something else they like. They become torn between the two pieces like a dog placed between two pieces of meat. It doesn't want to lose one piece while going for the other.

Most of us think we are living well. We convince ourselves that what we are doing is good for us, or we fret over the fact that we aren't. Sometimes we think our fretting is good for us. We are all mistaken.

The one who finds a secure place to work is blessed. Here is what makes a secure choice of worthwhile work: the desire to do something good for others. The more concerned you are with your own interests, the less good you may be doing.

All of us really want to be secure. The more things we love, the more easily we can be insecure. Suppose someone says to you, "I am going to hurt you. I am going to destroy your peace of mind. I am going to tell some bad things about you." That person will be as upset and disturbed as you are. Your spirit is exposed to as many hazards as are the things you love.

Because of physical needs and anxieties, you let the world in. Now you are anxious because you have the world.

—Guigo I: *Meditations*

Day 9—Evening

A Queen's Humble Prayer

Set your minds on things above, not on earthly things.
Colossians 3:2

Lord Jesus, help me to want what is most pleasant to you. You know what is best for me. Give what you will, when the right time comes, and in the quantity you prefer. Do with me as you please. Put me where you will. I am in your hands. I am your servant. I am ready to do whatever you command. You are the true peace of my heart and the perfect rest of my soul.

If you want me to be in light, I will praise you. If you want me to be in darkness, I will also praise you.

If you comfort me, I will bless you. If you allow me to be troubled, I will bless you.

O Lord, make possible by your grace that which is impossible by my nature.

Sometimes I think I am going to hold together, but when a little trouble comes it tears me apart. Good Lord, you know my weakness, my frailty. Have mercy on me.

—Catherine Parr: *Prayers and Meditations*

Day 10—Morning

Eyes of Faith

Because you have seen me, you have believed; blessed are those who have not seen and yet have believed. *John 20:29*

There is a supernatural dimension to everything. The most ordinary object and the most common-place event have a divine quality. Everything in life is a stone that builds a heavenly structure. If we are blind to this and live only according to what we can see and touch, we will stumble stupidly through a dark maze.

When we live by faith we see things another way. Those who trust only their physical senses will not perceive the riches that hide beneath outward appearances. If you see the hand of God in ordinary events, even in disasters, you will accept whatever comes your way with respect and pleasure. You will welcome things that terrify others. They may be clothed in rags, but you will respect the majesty hidden beneath those rags.

Think of God's poverty as he lay crying and trembling on some hay in a manger! If you were to ask the citizens of Bethlehem their opinions of the baby Jesus, you would get ordinary responses. If he had been born in a palace among all the splendor of a prince, people would have been eager to honor him. Not so with a child in a stable.

Now go ask Mary, Joseph, the shepherds, and the magi. They will tell you that in this absolute poverty they see something beyond words that is the glory of God. It is the very things which cannot be perceived by our senses that nourish and en-large faith. Seeing less, we believe more.

—Jean-Pierre de Caussade:
Abandonment to Divine Providence

Day 10—Evening

Really Praying the Lord's Prayer

When you pray, do not keep on babbling like pagans, for they think they will be heard because of their many words. *Matthew 6:7*

When I repeat the Lord's Prayer, my love causes me to desire to understand who this Father is, and who this Master is that taught us the prayer.

You are wrong if you think you already know who he is. We should think of him every time we say his prayer. Human frailty may interfere with this. When we are sick or our heads are tired, no matter how hard we try we may not be able to concentrate. If we are going through some stormy times we may be too distressed to pay attention to what we are saying. As hard as we try, we just can't do it.

Imagine that Jesus taught this prayer to each one of us individually and that he continues to explain it to us. He is always close enough to hear us. To pray the Lord's Prayer well there is one thing you need to do. Stay near the side of the Master who taught it to you.

—Teresa of Avila: *The Way of Perfection*

Day 11—Morning

Adversity As Friend

It was good for me to be afflicted so that I might learn your decrees. *Psalm 119:71*

Sometimes it is good for us to have trouble and crosses to bear. Adversity can return us to our senses. It can remind us that we are here as refugees, and that we must not place our trust in anything belonging to the world.

It is good that people sometimes misunderstand us. They may have a poor opinion of us even when our intentions are good. Such experiences lead us toward humility and protect us from conceit. We look for God more diligently when we are in difficulty. Our inner life grows stronger when we are under attack.

If you will fully establish yourself in God, you will not need the consolation of others. When we are troubled with temptation and evil thoughts, then we see clearly the great need we have of God, since without him we can do nothing good. Then with weariness and sorrow we may "desire to depart and be with Christ" (Philippians 1:23), for we understand that absolute security and peace do not exist in this world.

—Thomas á Kempis: *The Imitation of Christ*

Almost Blind

Without faith it is impossible to please God, because anyone who comes to him must believe that he exists and that he rewards those who earnestly seek him. *Hebrews 11:6*

If someone is almost blind, that person has little desire for a guide. Seeing a little bit, we figure it is best to travel in the direction that is most appealing. The alternatives are dimly perceived and uninviting. We can even lead a guide astray by insisting that we take a particular route.

This is the way it is when the soul leans upon its own knowledge. Perhaps there was a little feeling or experience of God. That may be an important blessing, but no matter how great it may have been, it is still very much different from what God is. Continue down that path and you may either be lead astray or bump into a dead end. *Faith* is the true guide of the soul.

Union with God is not the result of understanding, experience, feeling, or imagination. Isaiah and Paul both say, "No eye has seen, no ear has heard, no mind conceived what God has prepared for those who love him" (1 Corinthians 2:9; Isaiah 64:4). A soul is hampered from attaining this high state of union with God when it clings to any mental or emotional process of its own.

—John of the Cross: *Ascent of Mount Carmel*

A Valuable Lesson

Then you will know the truth, and the truth will set you free. *John 8:32*

If we take revenge, we are doing something to another person that we dislike for ourselves. We frequently get even by telling the truth with the intention of poisoning another life. For this reason we do not welcome the truth for ourselves.

Curiously, the cruel comments of enemies can be beneficial if we will accept them with humility. If someone accuses an adulterer of being an adulterer, the words may be spoken viciously, but the adulterer is hearing only what ought to be admitted anyway. It should be accepted without hesitation. The truth is more useful than the motive.

Truth brings life and salvation. Feel compassion for anyone who does not welcome it. That person may be missing out on the best God offers.

Here are the mistakes we make when we speak the truth. Sometimes we want our words to sting. At other times we want to please others, speaking the truth as if we were telling lies or flattering.

Speak the truth, not in order to upset or please someone, but to do another person good. Don't say anything at all if it would hurt.

—Guigo I: *Meditations*

Day 12—Evening

Taught by a Hickory Stick

You have forgotten that the Scriptures say to God's children, "When the Lord punishes you, don't make light of it, and when he corrects you, don't be discouraged. The Lord corrects the people he loves and disciplines those he calls his own." *Hebrews 12:5-8, CEV*

The best teachers are trouble and affliction. These alone give us understanding.

How can we feel God's goodness when nothing has troubled us and no danger hangs over our heads? These are the things God can help. If we are in good and perfect health do we need a physician? If we are relaxed and in no peril, why would we ever call for help?

As far as I can see, this is the chief reason why God always sharply schools those whom he loves most dearly. The troublesome hazards are effective schoolmasters. An ancient Greek proverb asserts that wisdom can be struck into a student. We are never more holy than when we bear some grievous cross.

—John Fox: *Christ Jesus Triumphant*

Day 13—Morning

Spiritual Combat

Follow the Lord's rules for doing his work, just as an athlete either follows the rules or is disqualified and wins no prize. *2 Timothy 2:5, TLB*

If you want the highest degree of spiritual perfection, you will need to wage constant warfare against yourself. It will take all your strength. Prepare for combat. You will need all the determination and courage you can muster.

No war is fought with greater fierceness than spiritual combat. We are both friend and foe. Both sides are equal. A victory gained is therefore very pleasing to God.

Whoever has the courage to control passions, subdue appetites, and repulse even the weakest inclinations of self-will performs meritorious action in the sight of God. Without this victory there is little glory even in the severest discipline, the greatest austerity, or the conversion of a multitude of sinners.

We need to start with ourselves. What does God expect of us?

Begin by equipping yourself with four weapons that are necessary for victory in spiritual combat:

- distrust yourself
- have confidence in God
- use your body and mind properly
- pray

—Lawrence Scupoli: *The Spiritual Combat*

By their fruit you will recognize them. Do people
pick grapes from thornbushes, or figs from thistles?
Matthew 7:16

Where there is love and wisdom, there is neither
fear nor ignorance.

Where there is patience and humility, there is
neither anxiety nor anger.

Where there is poverty and joy, there is neither
greed nor covetousness.

Where there is quiet and meditation, there is
neither care nor waste.

Where there is compassion and discretion,
there is neither excess nor indifference.

Where the fear of the Lord guards the door, the
enemy cannot enter.

—Francis of Assisi: *Admonitions*

One Day at a Time

For I know my transgressions, and my sin is always before me. *Psalm 51:3*

The rising of devotion in an ordinary soul is like the dawning of a new day. Darkness is not driven away immediately. Light comes in small increments, moment by moment. The saying is that a slow cure is best. Sicknesses of the soul are like those of the body. They come galloping in on horseback, but depart slowly on foot.

Have courage and be patient. Many see themselves as still imperfect after trying to be devout for a long time. They become discouraged and are tempted to give up. The opposite temptation is far more hazardous. Some figure everything is fixed on the first day! They have scarcely begun. They want to fly without wings. They are taking a great risk of relapse if they stop seeing the doctor too soon.

Purging the soul is a lifetime effort. There is no reason to be upset by our imperfections. Perfection is nothing more than fighting against them. How can we resist them unless we see them? How can we overcome them unless we face them?

—Francis de Sales: *The Devout Life*

Have you considered my servant Job? *Job 1:8*

It is a valuable thing for us to experience the valleys as well as the peaks. God wants us to know that he is with us in both good times and bad. For our spiritual benefit we are sometimes left to ourselves. We may be allowed to suffer misery. Both happiness and sadness are expressions of the same divine love. Of all the pains that lead to salvation, the greatest is to see your love suffer.

All of us experience a wonderful mixture of both well-being and woe. It is necessary for us to fall. If we did not fall, we would have the wrong idea about ourselves. Eventually we will understand that we are never lost to God's love. At no time are we ever less valuable in God's sight. Through failure we will clearly understand that God's love is endless. Nothing we can do will destroy it.

—Julian of Norwich: *Revelations of Divine Love*

Avoid Pride

Though the Lord is on high, he looks upon the lowly, but the proud he knows from afar. *Psalm 138:6*

It is after a soul-humbling day—or a time of trouble when the soul is lowest—that we have free access to God. The delight of God is in "those who have humble and contrite hearts, who tremble at [God's] word" (Isaiah 66:2, NLT). And God is the delight of such souls! Where the pleasure is mutual there will be free admittance, warm welcome, and easy conversation.

God denies access to a proud soul. "God opposes the proud but gives grace to the humble" (1 Peter 5:5; Proverbs 3:34). A proud mind is conceited. A humble mind finds self-esteem in God and holy aspirations. These two forms of high-mindedness are at opposite poles.

Most wars are between prince and prince, and not between prince and plowman. Are you puffed up with pride? Do you welcome the praise of others? Do you seek the highest honors? Do you become angry when your word or will is crossed? Can you not serve God in a low place as well as high? Do you enjoy celebrity? Are you unaware of the deceitfulness and wickedness of your heart? Are you more ready to defend your innocence than to confess your fault?

If these things describe your heart, you are a proud person. It is not likely you will have any familiarity with God. You make yourself a god. You are your own idol. How could you possibly have your heart in heaven? You might speak a few proper words, but your heart does not understand what you are saying.

—Richard Baxter: *The Saints' Everlasting Rest*

Day 15—Evening

Quiet Inspiration

After the earthquake came a fire, but the Lord was not in the fire. And after the fire came a gentle whisper. *1 Kings 19:12*

The Scriptures say without hesitation that God's Spirit lives in us, gives us life, speaks to us in silence, inspires us, and that it is so much a part of us that we are *united* with the Lord in Spirit. This is basic Christian teaching.

The Spirit of God is the soul of our soul! We are blind if we think that we are alone in the interior sanctuary. God is actually more present in this place than we are. We are constantly inspired, but we suppress the inspiration. God is always speaking to us, but the external noise of the world and the internal churning of our passions confuse us. We can't hear him speaking. Everything around us needs to be silent, and we must be quiet within. We need to focus our entire being to hear his soft whisper of a voice. The only ones who hear it are those who listen to nothing else.

—François de Fénelon: *Meditations and Devotions*

Day 16—Morning

Our Rights

Create in me a clean heart, O God; and renew a right
spirit within me. *Psalm 51:10, KJV*

There are many statements you need to avoid. "I
was right." "They did not have the right to do this
to me." God deliver us from such false notions of
what is right! Do you think it was right for Jesus
to suffer all those insults? Did the people who did
those bad things to a good man have the right to do
so? Why do we think we should only bear
crosses we think we have a right to expect?

Do you think that you have to put up with so
much now that you have the right not to bear any
more? How does the question of rightness even
enter this discussion? It has nothing to do with it.

When we are offended and hurt, there is nothing to complain about. We can share the dishonor
with Christ. Consider yourself fortunate to have
such an opportunity, and you will lack honor
neither in this life nor the next.

—Teresa of Avila: *The Way of Perfection*

He gives strength to the weary and increases the
power of the weak. *Isaiah 40:29*

We easily overestimate our own abilities. It is
not easy to spot the error in this.

Distrust of our own strength is a gift from
heaven. Sometimes we receive it through the inspiration of God. Sometimes it arrives with afflic-
tions and overwhelming temptations.

There are four things we need to do if we would
gain this spiritually healthy distrust of ourselves.

Meditate upon our own weakness. Admit that
we cannot accomplish the smallest good without
God's help.

Beg God for what God alone can give. Ac-
knowledge that we don't have it and that we can't
go somewhere and get it. Let's fall down at the
feet of our Lord and plead with him to grant our
request.

Gradually discard the illusions of our own
mind, our tendency to sin, and begin to see the
overwhelming, yet hidden, obstacles that sur-
round us.

As often as we commit a fault, we must take
inventory of our weaknesses. God permits us to
fall only in order to help us gain deeper insight
into ourselves.

God permits us to sin more or less grievously
in proportion to our pride. Every time we commit
a fault, we should earnestly ask God to enlighten
us. Ask him to help you see yourself as you are in
his sight.

Presume no more on your own strength. Otherwise, you will stumble again over the same stone.

—Lawrence Scupoli: *The Spiritual Combat*

Daily Essentials

We make our own plans, but the Lord decides where we will go. *Proverbs 16:9, CEV*

Christians ought to be as virtuous inside as they appear outside to others. No, they should be *better* in their heart than on the surface. Because God sees every part of us, we should be reverent before him and live as pure as angels in his sight.

Every day pray, "Help me, O Lord God! These are my good intentions in your service. Let me begin this day to settle down to the serious business of living a pure life, for what I have done so far is nothing."

The firmer we stick to our purpose, the more we will advance. If the one who tries the hardest frequently fails, what will become of the less enthusiastic? Remember that our best intentions do not depend upon us for fulfillment, but upon God. We are to rely on him for success in everything.

Even if we do the best we can, we will still fail many times. Yet we must always plan something definite, plot a course, especially as we battle our greatest personal weaknesses.

Determine a plan of action in the morning, and then evaluate yourself at night. How have you behaved today? What were your words, your deeds, your thoughts?

—Thomas á Kempis: *The Imitation of Christ*

Day 17—Evening

Forgiveness for Everything

If we confess our sins, [Jesus] is faithful and just and will forgive us our sins and purify us from all unrighteousness. *1 John 1:9*

There are none so wicked that they cannot have a remedy. What is that? Enter into your own heart and search its secrets. Consider your own life. How have you spent your days? If you find some ugliness in yourself, what will you do? Ask God to forgive you. You will surely be heard. Your sins will be forgiven. God will be true to his promise. He sent his only Son into this world to save sinners like you.

Consider the great love of God the Father. Amend your life. Avoid temptation. If you will do this, you may be sure that though you have done all the sins in the book they will neither hurt nor condemn you. The mercy of God is greater than all the sins in the world.

—Hugh Latimer: *Fruitful Sermons*

Day 18—Morning

A Personal Testimony

He has determined the times of their existence and the limits of their habitation, so that they might search for God, in the hope that they might feel for him and find him—yes, even though he is not far from any of us.
Acts 17:27, PHILLIPS

For more than forty years my continual concern has been to be always with God, and to do nothing, say nothing, and think nothing which may displease him. I have had no other motive for this than love of God.

I am now so accustomed to that Divine Presence that I am continually nourished by it. My soul has been filled with constant joy. Sometimes I have had to force myself not to let it show too much on the outside.

If I become a little too absent from the Divine Presence, as sometimes happens when I am busy, God soon makes himself felt in my soul and calls me back.

God's treasure is like an infinite ocean, and yet a little wave of emotion, passing with the moment, is enough for many. But when God finds a soul filled with a living faith, he pours into it his grace and good favor. They flow into the soul the way a torrent that has been stopped in its course for a while by some debris spreads its pent-up flood waters.

We often stop this torrent by the little value we give it. Make the most of your opportunity. Redeem the time that is lost. Maybe you don't have much left. Remember, in the spiritual life, failure to advance is going backward.

—Brother Lawrence:
The Practice of the Presence of God

Day 18—Evening

Trust God

Offer right sacrifices and trust in the Lord. *Psalm 4:5*

The best way to gain divine assistance is to place complete confidence in God.

With great humility and faith, contemplate the enormous power and wisdom of God. Nothing is too difficult for him. His goodness is unlimited. He is always ready to give those who love him the necessities for their spiritual life, and for gaining a complete victory over themselves. The only thing required of us is that we turn to him with complete confidence. What could be more reasonable?

For about thirty-three years Jesus, the Good Shepherd, looked for lost sheep in difficult terrain. Ultimately, it cost him his life. Is it possible for such a devoted shepherd to ignore a returning stray? Would it matter if the sheep had only a weak intention of following him? No. He would look on it with pity, listen to its cries, and take it up upon his own shoulders to return it to the flock.

Remember what the Holy Scriptures tell us in a thousand different places. No one who puts trust in God will be defeated.

Before attempting to do anything good, think about your own weakness and the infinite power, wisdom, and goodness of God. Balance what you fear about yourself with your faith in God.

—Lawrence Scupoli: *The Spiritual Combat*

Now is your time of grief, but I will see you again and
you will rejoice, and no one will take away your joy.
John 16:22

If you are caught in a fault you must certainly
humble yourself and admit your responsibility. If
you are the target of an unjust accusation, politely
deny your guilt. You owe it to both truth and your
neighbor. If you continue to be accused after you
have made a true and legitimate explanation,
don't let that bother you. There is no need to try
to force anyone to agree with your explanation.
After you discharge your duty to truth, then discharge your duty to humility.

The truly patient person neither whines nor
seeks pity. If that person must speak of his sufferings he will use a normal tone of voice and not
exaggerate. If that person is extended pity for
something he does not suffer, he will not accept
it. This way he keeps peace between truth and
patience.

—Francis de Sales: *The Devout Life*

Day 19—Evening

Why Love God?

How great is the love the Father has lavished on us, that we should be called children of God! *1 John 3:1*

You have asked me to tell you why and how God is to be loved. God himself is the reason why. Without limit is how.

For the wise, that is answer enough.

But now I will speak more elaborately, if less profoundly, for the benefit of less agile minds.

There are two reasons for loving God. First, there is no one more worthy of your love. Second, no one can return more in response to your love.

God deserves our love because he first loved us. His love for us was genuine because he sought nothing for himself. See the object of his love: enemies. "For if, when we were God's enemies, we were reconciled to him through the death of his Son, how much more, having been reconciled, shall we be saved through his life!" (Romans 5:10). God's love was unconditional.

How much did he love? The answer is in John's Gospel: "For God so loved the world that he gave his one and only Son, that whoever believes in him shall not perish but have eternal life" (John 3:16). The Son, speaking of himself, said, "The greatest way to show love for friends is to die for them" (John 15:13, CEV). We, the wicked, then, should love the Righteous One in return.

—Bernard of Clairvaux: *On Loving God*

Malicious Gossip

I am the Lord, the one who encourages you. Why are you afraid of mere humans? They dry up and die like grass. *Isaiah 51:12,* CEV

It is impossible to satisfy everyone. Paul said, "I try to find common ground with everyone" (1 Corinthians 9:22, NLT). And yet he said, "I care very little if I am judged by you or by any human court; indeed, I do not even judge myself" (1 Corinthians 4:3).

He did everything he could to lead others to Christ, but he still had plenty of detractors. Here is how Paul preserved his sanity: he turned it all over to God who knows everything.

When necessary, Paul faced those who tried to raise their own status by climbing over him. He answered their charges with humility and patience in order to protect others who might be hurt by his silence.

What power does anyone have to injure you with words? He hurts himself, not you. And he will not be able to escape God's judgment, regardless of who he is. Keep God in sight, and if anyone condemns you, ignore it.

Stay near God and don't worry about what others think of you. It is a good thing to suffer such judgment.

—Thomas á Kempis: *The Imitation of Christ*

Happiness

God blesses those people whose hearts are pure. They will see him! God blesses those people who make peace. They will be called his children! *Matthew 5:8-9, CEV*

The pure of heart are those who care nothing for earthly things and always look for heavenly things. They never stop adoring and contemplating the living God with a pure heart and mind.

The genuine peacemakers are those who remain at peace in their souls and bodies when they suffer in this world for the love of our Lord Jesus Christ.

Happy is the person who bears with neighbors, understanding their frail natures, as much as he would want to be borne with by them.

Happy is that devout person who experiences no pleasure or joy except in holy conversation and the works of the Lord, and who uses these means to lead others to the love of God.

Happy is the servant who never speaks merely to get a reward, who always carefully considers what to say. . . .

Happy is that brother who loves his brother as much when he is sick and not able to help him as he loves him when he is well and able to carry part of the burden. Happy is the brother who loves his brother as much when he is far away from him as he does when he is close by.

—Francis of Assisi: *Admonitions*

White Lies

You use your mouth for evil and harness your tongue to deceit. *Psalm 50:19*

Is it ever necessary to lie? Some think so. Even in religious matters it seems good to them to speak falsely. I believe every lie is a sin, though it may be a matter of degree. The intention and the topic need to be considered. Telling a lie in an attempt to be helpful is not the same as deliberate wickedness. Speaking falsely when you really think you are telling truth is not lying. In this case you are yourself deceived. It is rashness, not prevarication, when we accept as true what is false.

We lie when we speak the truth, if we actually thought it was a falsehood. Our intention was to lie. Consider the intentions rather than the content. We lie when we have one thought secured in our heart and another prepared for our tongue.

Some lies do no harm. It is a small thing. Good may result. But it is a mistake to deny that evil is bad, or to approve something false as though it were true, or to disapprove the truth as though it were false, or to hold what is certain as if it were uncertain, or the opposite. It is one thing to suppose that a particular road is the right one when it is not. It is something else entirely when that wrong road leads to something good.

—Augustine: *Enchiridion*

Where can I go from your Spirit? Where can I flee from your presence? *Psalm 139:7*

Here are the secrets of intimacy with God:

- Renounce everything that does not lead to God.
- Become accustomed to a continual conversation with him in freedom and simplicity.
- Speak to him every moment.
- Ask him to tell you what to do when you are not sure.
- Get busy with it when you plainly see what he requires of you.
- Offer your activity to him even before you do it.
- Give God thanks when you accomplish something.

The depth of your spirituality does not depend upon *changing* the things you do but in doing for God what you ordinarily do for yourself.

The biggest mistake is to think that a time of prayer is different from any other time. It is all one. Prayer is experiencing the presence of God. There should be no change when a time of formal prayer ends. Continue with God. Praise and bless him with all your energy.

—Brother Lawrence:
The Practice of the Presence of God

You are tempted in the same way that everyone else is tempted. But God can be trusted not to let you be tempted too much, and he will show you how to escape from your temptations. *1 Corinthians 10:13, CEV*

There is a vast difference between being tempted and yielding to it. And yet, if I know in advance that certain places will tempt me and I go there anyway, I am guilty of each temptation that comes my way.

The way to deal with temptations is to look away from them and at the Lord. If you are still subject to them, continue to resist. There is no sin as long as you say "No."

For every great temptation there will be many small ones. Wolves and bears are more dangerous than flies, but we are bothered most by the latter. You may never murder anyone, but you will certainly become angry. You may avoid adultery, but it is not easy to control your eyes. You may never steal anything from your neighbor, but you may covet it.

Let these flies and gnats buzz around you. Instead of fighting with them, do the very opposite of what the temptation is suggesting. For instance, if you are tempted to be vain, think about the troubles of others. If you are greedy, remember how death will take it all away from you, and then go give something away or pass up a profit. Make the effort and you will be hardened against future temptations.

—Francis de Sales: *The Devout Life*

God is our refuge and strength, an ever-present help in trouble. *Psalm 46:1*

God speaks: My child, do not be worn out by the work you are doing for me. Let no setback discourage you. I will give you strength. Remember, you will not be working here forever. If you will wait a little while, things will change.

Keep going, then. Work faithfully in my garden, and I will be your wages. Write, read, sing, mourn, be silent, and pray. Take all blows gladly. The kingdom of heaven is worth all this and much more.

A Christian responds: Heavenly Father, the time has come for me to be tested. It is proper that I should now suffer something for your sake. Before time began you knew this hour would come. Outwardly, I will be tormented; inwardly, I will be with you. For a little while, I will be a failure and an object of scorn. Go down with me Father, so I may rise with you in the dawning of a new light.

Such humbling is good for me, Lord. It helps me throw away haughtiness and pride. It is valuable that "I endure scorn for your sake, and shame covers my face" (Psalm 69:7). This makes me turn to you for comfort rather than to others. Thank you for this painful challenge. You know how troubled times can scour away the rust of sin. Do with me as you choose.

> O Lord,
> let me know what is worth knowing,
> love what is worth loving,
> praise what pleases you,
> honor what is worthy in your sight,
> and avoid all that is evil.

—Thomas á Kempis: *The Imitation of Christ*

The Divine Orchardist

I am the true vine and my Father is the gardener. He cuts off every branch in me that bears no fruit, while every branch that does bear fruit he prunes so that it will be even more fruitful. *John 15:1*

Consider an orchard in spring. See how the trees are taking on new life. Soon they will blossom and bear fruit. It is good to think of your soul as such a place. Imagine the Lord walking in it. Ask him to increase the fragrance of the little virtuous buds that are beginning to appear. Beg him to keep them alive until they can bloom to his glory. Invite him to prune away whatever he thinks needs to go. The trees will be better if he does.

A time will come to the soul when it is like an overgrown orchard. Everything seems dry and lifeless. It is hard to believe it was ever thriving and flourishing. The soul suffers many trials. The poor orchardist thinks that it is out of control and lost.

This is the proper time for cultivation. Remove the weeds. Root out sickly plants. Make room for the healthy trees. If we do this we can gain much humility, and then the blossoms will come again.

—Teresa of Avila: *The Life of Teresa of Jesus*

A Prayer for the Earth

My job was to plant the seed in your hearts, and Apollos watered it, but it was God, not we, who made it grow. The ones who do the planting or watering aren't important, but God is important because he is the one who makes the seed grow. *1 Corinthians 3:6-7,* NLT

In the beginning you commanded the earth, O Lord, to yield green grass, herbs, and trees. Their seeds and fruits were food for your creatures living on the earth. To humans you gave dominion over everything, vegetable, animal, and mineral. We are to receive them with thanksgiving.

Because you alone are the Creator and Maker of all things, we seek your blessing. We may plant and water, but you give the increase. We pray that the earth may give her fruit abundantly. Bless the labors of our hands. We know we do not feed ourselves. We are the sheep of your pasture (Psalm 100:3).

You feed us. You provide the earth. You water our gardens. You break up the clods and make them soft with rain. You make things multiply. You crown the year with your bountifulness. Your footsteps drop nourishment. You make the wilderness lush.

You cause wells to spring up in the valleys and rivers to run among the hills. You make "grass to grow for the cattle. You cause plants to grow for people to use. You allow them to produce food from the earth—wine to make them glad, olive oil as lotion for their skin, and bread to give them strength" (Psalm 104:14-15, NLT).

If our barns are full, it is because you have blessed us. You have opened your hand.

—Thomas Becon: *The Flower of Godly Prayers*

Day 24—Morning

Knowing the Unknowable

Who among the gods is like you, O Lord? Who is like you—majestic in holiness, awesome in glory, working wonders? *Exodus 15:11*

If we attempt to comprehend God, the God we think we understand is not God. The human mind is not large enough to investigate God. We will be led into errors. The deeper we dig, the farther we go away from God.

God's presence and activity are beyond our ability to comprehend. We can accept them with faith. We can be deeply thankful for them. But there is no way we can grasp them, describe them, and explain them. We are not even able to understand our own motives and behavior. How can we expect to know the mind of God?

We enjoy bread without understanding how the wheat grew. We drink our fill of water at a riverbank without having any idea of its source. We protect our eyes from brightness in order to see things in daylight, but we have no way to figure how much light there is in the sun. A baby drinks from its mother's breast but cannot think how the breast got there.

The closer we are to God, the less we know about God.

—Pseudo-Macarius: *Homilies*

Day 24—Evening

Secret Prayer

When you pray, go into your room, close the door and pray to your Father, who is unseen. *Matthew 6:6*

Avoid all worldly praise and profit when you pray. Really pray! Christ does not forbid open prayers. Sometimes we need a place to come together for group prayer. We can share thanks or requests to God. We can pray for peace and safety as a community. We have common interests in weather and fruits. In a congregation we can pray that we may be spared pestilence and plague.

But we need a secret place of prayer. This will keep us from showing off. It leaves us free to use any words we please. If we want to make gestures that increase our devotion no one else will know.

Go boldly to God. He desires your prayers and has commanded you to pray. He promises to hear you, not because you are good but because he is good.

—William Tyndale:
Exposition upon the Sermon on the Mount

Day 25—Morning

Heavenly Music

Shout for joy to the Lord, all the earth, burst into jubilant song with music; make music to the Lord with the harp . . . and the sound of singing, with trumpets and the blast of the ram's horn—shout for joy before the Lord. *Psalm 98:4-6*

Nothing less than God can fill our soul. Its capacity is designed for God alone. If we try to fill it with earthly things, we will never be satisfied. Lovers of God will be at peace when they are filled with God through desire and meditation.

Singing is a delightful way in which our spirits can ascend to the pleasures of heaven. We are swept away by a beautiful hymn flowing with joy.

Once I was sitting in a chapel, singing the Psalms as well as I could in the evening before supper. It seemed as though I could hear stringed instruments playing above me. With my prayers I reached out to these heavenly sounds. I experienced a blending of the internal melodies I was improvising with the heavenly harmonies. My meditation was transformed into music.

I am not saying that this is for everyone. If the gift is given, let the one receiving it enjoy it.

—Richard Rolle: *The Fire of Love*

Day 25—Evening

Assembling a Choir

Praise the Lord with the harp; make music to him on the ten-stringed lyre. Sing to him a new song; play skillfully, and shout for joy. *Psalm 33:2-3*

I place before my inward eyes everything there is about me—my body, soul, and abilities. I gather around me all the creatures which God ever created in heaven and on earth. I touch each element, calling it by name. I include the birds of the air, the beasts of the forests, the fish of the sea, the leaves and grass of the earth, the innumerable grains of sand, and all the little specks of dust that dance in the sunbeams. I embrace every little drop of water which falls as dew, snow, or rain.

I wish that each of these had a sweetly sounding musical instrument made of my heart's inmost blood, the sounding of which might send up to our dear and gentle God a new and lofty strain of praise.

And then the loving arms of my soul stretch out and extend themselves toward the innumerable multitude of all creation. In the same way that a choral director can stir up singers, I would incite them to sing joyously, offering up their hearts to God.

—Heinrich Suso: *The Life of Blessed Henry*

Flatterers

Honest correction is appreciated more than flattery.
Proverbs 28:23, CEV

There are three kinds of flatterers.

The first kind praises and encourages someone's good behavior. But they overdo it. They make a person feel better than they really are. Lavish praise is the first type of flattery. It is evil enough.

The second kind takes an openly soiled reputation that is beyond denial and makes light of it. "You are not the first person to do this. Many others do things that are worse."

The third kind of flatterer is the worst of all. They praise an evil person's conduct. To a knight who has robbed the poor they will say, "That's not a bad thing to do. Prune a willow and it will sprout even better." Such misguided flatterers actually blind the ones who listen to them. They cloak a foul odor with perfume. This is too bad. If they smelled it, it would make them sick. They would hurry to confession and avoid it in the future.

—Anonymous: *A Guide for Anchoresses*

A Special Prayer

Hasten, O God, to save me; O Lord, come quickly to help me. *Psalm 70:1*

This verse from Psalm 70 fits every mood and disposition of human nature. It covers every temptation and every situation. It contains an appeal to God, a plain disclosure of faith, a reverent anticipation, a contemplation on our weakness, a trusting in God's answer, and an assurance of God's providence.

This verse is an unbeatable defense. It is a shield, a suit of armor. Souls drowning in a sea of anxiety will find it to be the cure for despair. It reminds us of God's constant watchfulness. If life is sweet and one is happy, it warns against complacency. It reminds everyone that we keep what we have won only with God's protection.

Whatever the condition of our spiritual life, we need to use this verse. It reminds us that we need God to help us in both prosperity and suffering, in happiness and sorrow. Our frail nature cannot survive in either state without God's help.

—John Cassian: *Conference Ten on Prayer*

Day 27—Morning

Human Nature and God's Grace

He lifted me out of the slimy pit, out of the mud and mire; he set my feet on a rock and gave me a firm place to stand. *Psalm 40:2*

Human nature and grace move in opposite directions. Here is how to tell the difference between them:

- Human nature is tricky and often misleads and traps. It only cares about itself. Grace avoids guile and cares about God.
- Human nature puts up a fight and dies reluctantly. It is not easily changed or held under control. Grace brings orderliness and does not abuse freedoms.
- Human nature hates to be shamed or rejected. Grace is pleased to endure such things in the name of God and accepts them as special favors when they come.
- Human nature desires exotic and exclusive things. Grace enjoys the ordinary.
- Human nature is greedy and finds receiving more blessed than giving. Grace is generous to the poor and content with little.
- Human nature wants recognition and admiration for good deeds. Grace hides its good works and gives all praise to God.

—Thomas á Kempis: *The Imitation of Christ*

Simple Openness

The law of the Lord is perfect, reviving the soul. The statutes of the Lord are trustworthy, making wise the simple. *Psalm 19:7*

Since God is always speaking within all of us, no one is exempt. He speaks within the most incorrigible sinner. And he speaks in the hearts of the scholars who are too full of their own wisdom to listen to God. They depend entirely upon reason. They have a self-inflated notion of their ability.

I have often said that any common sinner who is beginning to be converted through honest love of God will understand more about this interior word of the Spirit than those who are set in their own wisdom. God wants to communicate with those who see themselves as wise, but they are too full of themselves to listen.

His presence is with the simple. Who are they? I have not met many. But God knows who they are, and he is pleased to live with them.

—François de Fénelon: *Meditations and Devotions*

Day 28—Morning

Prayer in a Time of Trouble

May the Lord answer you when you are in distress.
Psalm 20:1

The only ones who understand the power of prayer are those who have learned from experience.

It is important to pray in a time of extreme need. I know about this. Whenever I have prayed with passion, I have been heard. I have received more than I prayed for. Sometimes there was a delay, but the answer always came.

Prayer is a potent thing! God welcomes our prayers. There is no reason for us to hesitate. Trusting Christ's promises, we can pray with the assurance that God hears and answers.

God wants us to pray when we are in trouble. He may hide himself a little. We will have to go looking for him. Christ says, "Ask and it will be given to you; seek and you will find; knock and the door will be opened to you" (Matthew 7:7). If we intend to come to God, we must knock and then knock some more. We need to continue with much knocking at God's door.

—Martin Luther: *Table Talk*

Day 28 — Evening

Prayer for a Friend

If you fall, your friend can help you up. But if you fall without having a friend nearby, you are really in trouble. *Ecclesiastes 4:10,* CEV

A friend asked me to pray earnestly to God for him. He did not need to ask. I was going to pray for him quite naturally.

I went to the place where I prefer to pray alone and began to talk to the Lord in a foolish way. This often happens in spontaneous prayer. It is love that is speaking. My soul is transported. It becomes immersed in God. Love that understands it is in God forgets itself and speaks absurdities.

I recall that after I begged God with many tears for my friend, I said that even though I thought he was good, this wasn't enough. I wanted him to be exceptionally good. I said, "Lord, don't let me down. This man is able to be our friend."

O the goodness of God! You don't look at the words, but at the desires and the will with which they are spoken! How can you bear it when someone like me speaks so boldly to you? May you be blessed forever!

—Teresa of Avila: *Life*

Day 29—Morning

God's Humility and Ours

Unto us a child is born, unto us a son is given. *Isaiah 9:6, KJV*

In the birth of the Christ child, God "emptied himself" (Philippians 2:7) of his majesty and took on both an ordinary human body and the vulnerability and unimportance of a baby. This sacred childhood restored our innocence.

Are you an important person? Have you been successful? Are you proud of your status as a giant in this world? "Unless you change and become like little children, you will never enter the kingdom of heaven" (Matthew 18:3). Unless your proud head is bowed, you will not be able to enter through the door of humility. Let this shake your self-confidence. If we approach him haughtily, we will be cast out.

How can you still be proud, dust and ashes, after God has humbled himself? How can you still be great in your own eyes when you know God made himself a child? God emptied himself. Why are you puffed up? You are leading yourself astray.

If you want to be someone even greater than you are, gain more humility. The Greatest of All made himself Least of All. The holy and the humble see this and honor it. The secular and proud see it and are bewildered.

—Guerric of Igny: *Liturgical Sermons*

Day 29—Evening

A Time and Place to Pray

Arise, cry out in the night, as the watches of the night begin; pour out your heart like water in the presence of the Lord. *Lamentations 2:19*

If you want to pray, you must choose not only the right place but also the right time. Quiet time is best. The deep silence when others are asleep inspires natural prayer. Prayer is a secret thing at night. It is witnessed only by God. It is pleasing, untainted, modest prayer. There are no interruptions, no noise. It becomes pure prayer, sincere prayer. There is no trace of exhibitionism or human adulation.

—Bernard of Clairvaux: *On the Song of Songs*

The First Commandment

You shall have no other gods before me. *Exodus 20:3*

There are ways in which we worship false gods. It is possible to be so attached to a thing or a person as to turn it into an idol. Even though you don't say it with your mouth, you have an object of worship that is not God.

Another way to have a false god is to put your confidence in anything other than God. If you wish you were rich, or desire to have a certain friend or supporter, and think that this will bring you happiness and security, you may have taken a false god. The Lord is God alone. Our confidence is to be anchored in him alone.

Think about these false gods as weeds in your garden. Pull them out by the root. Set your heart on nothing that is not God. Love God with your whole heart. Do everything for his sake. And above all, *obey* God. For if we merely revere, love, and trust—but do not obey—God, we are making God into what we want; we are making him into a false god.

—Thomas Cranmer: *Catechismus*

Requests for Prayer

Jesus answered them, "It is not the healthy who need a doctor, but the sick." *Luke 5:31*

When people ask you to remember someone in prayer they will often say, "This is such a nice person!" That is like taking someone who is ill to the doctor and saying, "Make him well because he is so healthy!" Maybe what they mean by the "nice person" idea is that there may be a little hope for that individual's salvation.

Sometimes they will say, "Pray for so-and-so because this person has done good things on your behalf." I would prefer to pray for someone who has done me wrong. Such a person actually needs my prayers.

It is a good thing to pray for anyone who confesses and asks for forgiveness. It is even better to pray for someone who does not yet feel guilty about anything. Ask God to help them notice their sin. And pray also for those who know they are guilty but will not admit it. Maybe they are ashamed. Maybe they are actually enjoying their guilt. Ask God to help them.

—Guigo I: *Meditations*

Day 31—Morning
Slander

Let slanderers not be established in the land. *Psalm 140:11*

If you rob your neighbor of a good reputation, you have the obligation of making reparation. You can't enter heaven carrying someone else's property. Of all external possessions, a good name is most important. Slander is a form of murder.

With a single stroke of the tongue you can commit three murders. You kill your own soul, the soul of anyone who hears your slanderous comments, and the social life of your victim. It is spiritual homicide. Saint Bernard says that the slanderer has the devil on the tongue, and the one who listens to slander has the devil in the ear. A snake tongue is forked with two points. So also is the slanderer's tongue: It poisons the listener as well as the one being spoken against. . . .

People who preface slander with comments about doing "the right thing" or who make little private jokes are the most vicious slanderers of them all. "I really like him," they say. "In every other regard he is a fine man, but the truth must be told." "She was a nice girl, but she must have been caught at a weak moment." You can see what they are up to with these little tricks. The archer pulls the arrow back as near to himself as possible in order to put more force into the shot. Slanderous joking is the most cruel of all. Hemlock is not a quick poison by itself. There is time to take an antidote. When hemlock is taken with wine, there is no antidote for it. In the same way slander that might pass lightly in one ear and out the other, sticks in the mind when it is told with a funny story.

—Francis de Sales: *The Devout Life*

Day 31—Evening

A Daring Prayer

Let us then approach the throne of grace with confidence, so that we may receive mercy and find grace to help us in our time of need. *Hebrews 4:16*

I had some fun with God today! I dared to complain to him. I said:

> Explain to me, please, why you keep me in this miserable life. Why do I have to put up with it? Everything here interferes with my enjoyment of you. I have to eat and sleep and work and talk with everyone. I do it all for the love of you, but it torments me.
>
> And how is it that when there is a little break and I can have some time with you, you hide from me? Is this the way you show me mercy? If you love me, how can you do this to me? I honestly believe, Lord, that if it were possible for me to hide from you the way you hide from me, you would not allow it. But you are with me and see me always. Stop this, Lord! It hurts me because I love you so much.

I said these and other things to God. Sometimes love becomes foolish and doesn't make a lot of sense. The Lord puts up with it. May so good a King be praised! We wouldn't dare say these things to earthly kings!

—Teresa of Avila: *Life*

Day 32—Morning

Suffering As an Opportunity

I consider that our present sufferings are not worth
comparing with the glory that will be revealed in us.
Romans 8:18

I don't pray that you may be delivered from your
troubles. Instead, I pray that God will give you the
strength and patience to bear them. Comfort yourself with him who nails you to the cross. Happy
are those who suffer with him.

The world doesn't understand this. That's not
surprising. They suffer as lovers of the world and
not as lovers of Christ. They think that sickness is
a pain of nature and find nothing in it but grief and
distress. But it can be a consolation to those who
understand that God can use illness in mercy.

God is frequently closer to us in sickness than
in health. Put all of your trust in him and you will
soon be on the road to recovery. Medicine will
help you only to the degree God permits. When
pains come from God, only he can heal them.
Sometimes a disease of the body will cure a
sickness in the soul.

—Brother Lawrence:
The Practice of the Presence of God

The Lord is good, a refuge in times of trouble. He cares for those who trust in him. *Nahum 1:7*

Take your problems promptly to God. He could help you much faster if you were not so slow in turning to prayer, but you try everything else first.

Now that you have caught your breath and your trouble has passed, recuperate in God's mercies. God is near you to repair all damage and to make things better than before. Is anything too hard for God? Where is your faith? Stand strong in God. Have patience and courage. Comfort will come in time. Wait. He will come to you with healing. . . .

It is better for you to experience a little adversity than to have everything exactly as you choose. Otherwise, you may become mistakenly self-satisfied. What God has given, he can take away. He can return it again when he pleases. When God gives something to you, it is on loan. When he takes it back, he is not asking for anything that is yours. "Every good and perfect gift is from above, coming down from the Father of the heavenly lights, who does not change like shifting shadows" (James 1:17).

—Thomas á Kempis: *The Imitation of Christ*

Waking Up to God

Great is the Lord, and most worthy of praise. *Psalm 48:1*

We are only a fraction of your enormous creation, Lord, but we still want to praise you. You have made us for yourself and our hearts are restless until they rest in you.

Which comes first, knowing you or praying to you? Surely no one can pray to you who does not know you. And yet, maybe we need to pray before we can really know you. The faith you infused in me, Lord, cries out to you:

> O God, you are the greatest and the best, the strongest, the most merciful and just, absolutely concealed and absolutely present, beautiful, mysterious, never changing, but changing everything, never new, yet never old, always in action, yet always at rest, attracting all things to yourself but needing none, preserving and fulfilling and sheltering, conceiving and nourishing and ripening, continually seeking but lacking nothing, you love without the confusion of emotion, you are jealous, but without fear. You owe us nothing and yet you give to us as though you were indebted to us. You forgive what is due you, and yet lose nothing yourself.

After all of this, what have I said? What can anyone say when speaking of God?

—Augustine: *Confessions*

Desperate Times

I am worn out from groaning; all night long I flood my bed with weeping and drench my couch with tears. *Psalm 6:6*

With his complaints, David speaks to God in the Psalms as though he were talking to someone who is ignorant of what he is suffering. It seems as though David thinks God is not taking care of him and knows nothing of his problems.

But no matter how deep and dark the dungeon of desperation is, the eyes of faith can find plenty of goodness in God. The storm may not cease at once. It is enough to cast out this anchor of faith. God will surely preserve your ship.

—John Knox: *Exposition of the Sixth Psalm*

Day 34—Morning

God Is Not in the Details

Don't get involved in foolish, ignorant arguments that only start fights. The Lord's servants must not quarrel but must be kind to everyone. They must be able to teach effectively and be patient with difficult people.
2 Timothy 2:23-24, NLT

Avoid arguments about the trivial details of faith. You don't need a religion that is composed of opinions. People who dispute violently about the fine points of religion are usually the least acquainted with God. If your religion is all in your firmly held opinions, you will be loud and obnoxious. If your religion rests in the knowledge and love of God, you will communicate pleasantly and be an attractive representative. . . .

I wish you could defend every one of God's truths. But concentrate on the important things. The least controversial points are the ones that are most valuable to the soul. Study texts like this:

> Anyone who teaches anything different, and does not keep to the sound teaching which is that of our Lord Jesus Christ, the doctrine which is in accordance with true religion, is simply arrogant and must be full of self-conceit—with a craze for questioning everything and arguing about words. All that can come of this is jealousy, contention, abuse and wicked mistrust of one another; and unending disputes by people who are neither rational nor informed and imagine that religion is a way of making a profit. (1 Timothy 6:3-5, JB)

—Richard Baxter: *The Saints' Everlasting Rest*

Day 34—Evening

Why Pray?

Do not worry, saying, "What shall we eat?" or "What shall we drink?" or "What shall we wear?" For the pagans run after all these things, and your heavenly Father knows that you need them. *Matthew 6:31-32*

Some ask if God needs us as advisers. After all, if he already knows about our problems and is wise enough to know what we need, why bother to pray?

Anyone who asks such questions does not understand why the Lord taught us to pray. It is not so much for his sake as for ours.

Faithful people in the Bible were certain that God was merciful and kind. But the more they realized this, the more fervently they prayed. Elijah is one such example. He was confident that God would break a drought and send desperately needed rain. In his confidence he prayed anxiously with his face between his knees. In no way did he doubt God would send rain. He understood that it was his duty to lay his desires before God.

It is true that God is awake and watches over us continuously. Sometimes he will assist us even when we do not ask. But it is in our own best interests to pray constantly. When we do, we will begin to understand that it is God who is in charge. It will keep us free of evil desires because we will learn to place all our wishes in his sight. Most importantly, it will prepare us to understand that God is the giver, and we will be filled with genuine gratitude and thanksgiving. Our prayers remind us that all things flow from his hand.

There is no better thing than to pray for what God already wants to give.

—John Calvin: *Institutes*

Day 35—Morning

Seeking Perfection

Be perfect, therefore, as your heavenly Father is perfect. *Matthew 5:48*

Christian perfection is nothing to dread. There is pleasure in giving ourselves to one we love. There is a contentment which you will never discover by giving in to your passions, but which will certainly be yours if you give yourself up to God. It is not the satisfaction of the world, but it is nonetheless genuine. It is a quiet, calm peace. The world can neither give it nor take it away. If you have any doubt about it, try it yourself. "O, taste and see that the Lord is good" (Psalm 34:8, KJV).

Organize your time so that you can find a period every day for reading, meditation, and prayer. This will become easy when you truly love him. We never wonder what we will talk about. He is our friend. Our heart is open to him. We must be completely candid with him, holding nothing back. Even if there is nothing we care to say to him, it is a joy just to be in his presence.

Love is a far better sustainer than fear. Fear enslaves, but love persuades. Love takes possession of our soul, and we begin to want goodness for itself. God is a kind and faithful friend to those who sincerely become his friend.

—François de Fénelon: *Meditations and Devotions*

Day 35—Evening

Genuine Peace

Peace I leave with you; my peace I give you. I do not give to you as the world gives. *John 14:27*

Everyone wants peace, but very few care for the things that produce it. God's peace is with the humble and the gentle, and especially with the patient. If you will listen to God, and act accordingly, you will enjoy much peace.

Here is what to do. Care for nothing other than pleasing God. Do not judge others or meddle in things which do not concern you. Following this advice will spare you needless trouble. But remember that it is impossible to be entirely free of trouble and fatigue in this life.

Don't think that you have found true peace just because you feel no pain or have no enemies. Never think that life is perfect when you receive everything you want. Never consider yourself God's favorite child because you enjoy a great devotional life. That is not the way to true peace and spiritual growth.

Peace can be found in offering your whole heart to God. Forget your own will in great things and small things, thanking God equally for the pleasant and the unpleasant. Weigh everything in the same balance.

If you are strong enough to willingly suffer more and more without praising yourself, but always praising God's name, then you will be on the road to true peace. You will have the hope of seeing him in the everlasting joy of heaven.

—Thomas á Kempis: *The Imitation of Christ*

Day 36—Morning

In the Right Order

Two people were in debt to a moneylender. One of them owed him five hundred silver coins, and the other owed him fifty. Since neither of them could pay him back, the moneylender said that they didn't have to pay him anything. Which one of them will like him more? *Luke 7:41-42,* CEV

Love is not the cause of forgiveness. Forgiveness causes love. The more we are forgiven, the more we love.

If we fill our thoughts with sin and damnation and the wrath of God which condemns us before we are born, we cannot love God. We will hate him as a tyrant, and run away from him. But when the gospel of Christ demonstrates how God loves us first, forgives us, and has mercy on us, then we love again. As the saying goes, "Summer is near, because the trees blossom." The blossoms do not bring summer. Summer brings the blossoms.

—William Tyndale: *The Parable*

Love Directs Our Thoughts

Take captive every thought to make it obedient to
Christ. *2 Corinthians 10:5*

Gather, O Lord, my senses and the powers of
my soul together in yourself. Pardon me and
forgive me as often as I pray without concentrat-
ing on you. Many times I am not really at the place
where I am standing or sitting. My thoughts carry
me to some other place. I am where my thought
is. I love what I think about.

If I love heaven, I speak gladly of the things
of God.

If I love the world, I love to talk of worldly
things.

If I love the flesh, I imagine things that please
the flesh.

If I love my soul, I delight in talk about things
that are for my soul's health.

Whatever I love, I gladly hear and speak of it.
I fantasize about it. Jesus was right when he said,
"For where your treasure is, there your heart will
be also" (Matthew 6:21).

—Catherine Parr: *Prayers and Meditations*

Day 37—Morning

Knowing and Speaking

The kingdom of God is not a matter of talk but of power. *1 Corinthians 4:20*

Telling me that bread is made of wheat is not a difficult task. But can you tell me how to mix and bake a loaf of bread? The Christian gospel tells us about being freed of our passions. Jesus clearly tells us, "Do not resist an evil person. If someone strikes you on the right cheek, turn to him the other also. And if someone wants to sue you and take your tunic, let him have your cloak as well. If someone forces you to go one mile, go with him two miles" (Matthew 5:39-41). Can you tell me how to do that if you have not done it yourself?

Anyone who talks about spiritual things without any experience in them is like a person who is lost in the desert, dying with thirst. With a dry, parched throat and burning lips, she draws a picture of a water fountain. You can't tell me about the sweetness of honey until you have tasted some honey. If you try to tell me about the Christian life without any personal involvement in it, you will mislead me. You will tell me fictional things, mistaken things. The faith you have tried to sell me is nothing more than words. Your religion is just talk.

It is impossible to understand and serve truth unless you have that truth.

—Pseudo-Macarius: *Homilies*

When You Stumble

"Come now, let us reason together," says the Lord. "Though your sins are like scarlet, they shall be as white as snow; though they are red as crimson, they shall be like wool." *Isaiah 1:18*

You have committed a sin. It may have been from weakness or with malice. Don't panic. Go to God with humility and confidence. "Look what I can do, O Master. When I trust my own strength, I sin."

Let the Lord know you are sorry. Admit it may have been worse if he had not stopped you. Thank God. Love God. He will be generous toward you. Even though what you have done is offensive to him, he will reach out to help you.

Once you have asked God's pardon, don't begin to wonder whether or not he has actually forgiven you. This is a total waste of time, a sickness of the soul. It may seem like a good and reasonable question, but it is not. Fall into the mercy of God and return to your regular life as though the sin had not occurred.

Maybe you sin again in a short time. Don't let that shake your confidence in God. Return to him again and again. Each defeat will teach you to trust your own strength less and less.

—Lawrence Scupoli: *The Spiritual Combat*

Forgive us our debts, as we also have forgiven our debtors. *Matthew 6:12*

There are two causes of sin. Either we don't know what we ought to do or we refuse to do what we know we should. The first cause is ignorance. The second is weakness.

While we can fight against both, we will certainly be defeated unless God helps us. God can teach us what is right. As our knowledge of good and evil grows, God can help us to desire the better.

When we pray for forgiveness, we need to pray also that God will lead us away from sin. The psalmist sings, "The Lord is my light and my salvation" (Psalm 27:1). With light he takes away our ignorance. With salvation he strengthens us in weakness.

—Augustine: *Enchiridion*

Keeping Prayer on Track

Do not be quick with your mouth, do not be hasty in your heart to utter anything before God. God is in heaven and you are on earth, so let your words be few. *Ecclesiastes 5:2*

So you have difficulty with wandering thoughts in prayer! That's nothing new! You have a lot of company.

One way to remedy this is to tell God about it. Don't use a lot of fancy words or make your prayers too long. That in itself will destroy your attention. Pray like a poor, paralytic beggar before a rich man. Make it your *business* to keep your mind in the Presence of the Lord. If you have difficulty with that, don't fret about it. That will only make it worse. Bring your attention back to God in tranquility.

Another way to stay with a prayer is to keep your mind from wandering too far at other times of the day. Keep it strictly in the Presence of God. If you think of him a lot, you will find it easy to keep your mind calm in the time of prayer.

—Brother Lawrence:
The Practice of the Presence of God

Filling an Emptiness

While he was blessing them, he left them and was taken up into heaven. *Luke 24:51*

Lord, you began to perfect your apostles by taking away from them the very thing they didn't think they could do without—the actual presence of Jesus. You destroy in order to build. You take away everything in order to restore it many times over. This is the way you work. You do it differently than we would do it.

Once Christ was gone, you sent the Holy Spirit. Sometimes lacking is more powerful than having. Blessed are those who are deprived of everything. Blessed are those from whom Jesus is removed. The Holy Spirit, the Comforter, will come to them. He will comfort their sorrows and wipe away their tears.

But Lord, why isn't my life filled with this Spirit? It ought to be the soul of my soul, but it isn't. I feel nothing. I see nothing. I am both physically and spiritually lazy. My feeble will is torn between you and a thousand meaningless pleasures. Where is your Spirit? Will it ever arrive and "create in me a pure heart, O God" (Psalm 51:10)? Now I understand! Your Holy Spirit desires to live in an impoverished soul.

Come, Holy Spirit! There is no place emptier than my heart. Come. Bring peace.

—François de Fénelon: *Meditations and Devotions*

Day 39—Evening

The Light in the Darkness

Though I sit in darkness, the Lord will be my light.
Micah 7:8

The one who loves God remains entirely in light. However, if someone begins to perceive that the love of this world is false and temporary, and therefore prefers the love of God, that person will not instantly be brought into that light. There will be night for a while. It is not possible to move quickly from one light to another, from the love of the world to perfect love of God.

This spiritual night is a dividing line. It separates the two loves. It is a *good* night, a luminous darkness. It has turned away from the false love of this world and is coming closer to the true day of the love of Jesus. The passage through this night means your soul is almost there. This is what the prophet Micah means in chapter 7. When my soul is protected from the stirrings of sin, the Lord is our light.

Even so, this night of the soul can be distressing as well as comforting. The greater the change taking place, the greater the pain. The world is near and God seems far away. If this should happen for you, don't be discouraged. There is no need to struggle. Wait for God's grace. Live through the night quietly. Focus your attention on Jesus. Think only of him.

When your soul is truly free and desires only Christ, it is then in a good darkness. It is a darkness against false light. Jesus, who is both love and light, is in this darkness. It does not matter whether it is pleasant or unpleasant. Understand that it is a darkness before dawn.

—Walter Hilton: *The Scale of Perfection*

Day 40 —Morning

A Final Charge

You have made known to me the path of life; you will fill me with joy in your presence, with eternal pleasures at your right hand. *Psalm 16:11*

If birds stop beating their wings, they quickly fall to the ground. Unless your soul works at holding itself up, your flesh will drag it down.

You must renew your determination regularly.

Oddly, a spiritual crash leaves us lower than when we began.

Clocks need winding, cleaning, and oiling. Sometimes they need repair. Similarly, we must care for our spiritual life by examining and servicing our hearts at least annually.

There is plenty of time for other things. You do not have to do it all every day.

Stay with it. Time flies away. Keep your eyes on heaven. Don't throw it away for earthly things. Look at Jesus Christ and be faithful to him.

Live, Jesus! To whom, with the Father and the Holy Spirit, be all honor and glory, now and forevermore. Amen.

—Francis de Sales: *The Devout Life*

A Final Word

He has taken me to the banquet hall, and his banner over me is love. *Song of Songs 2:4*

In spite of our poor choices and spiritual blindness in this life, our courteous Lord continues to love us. We will bring him the most pleasure if we rejoice with him and in him.

When the end comes and we are taken for judgment above, we will then clearly understand in God the mysteries that puzzle us now. Not one of us will think to say, "Lord, if it had been some other way, all would be well."

We shall all say in unison, "Lord, bless you because it is all the way it is. It is well. Now we can honestly see that everything is done as you intended; you planned it before anything was ever made."

What is the meaning of it all? Listen carefully. Love is the Lord's meaning. Who reveals it? Love. Why does he reveal it? For love.

This is the only lesson there is. You will never learn another. Never. We began in love, and we shall see all of this in God forever.

—Julian of Norwich: *Showings*

Wish there were more than just 40 morning and evening readings?

These short readings have been taken from *Near To the Heart of God: Daily Readings from the Spiritual Classics*, compiled and prepared for the modern reader by Bernard Bangley. If you have appreciated this collection and would like even more—a full year of readings—order *Near To the Heart of God* (ISBN 0-87788-824-8) from your local bookstore or from Harold Shaw Publishers.

Here's what has been said about *Near To the Heart of God*:

> "An amazing collection of dynamic quotes from the masters in the long, spiritual tradition. In this neatly structured book of daily readings, each should be a shaft of light to enlighten the soul."—*Ben C. Johnson, professor of Christian Spirituality, Columbia Theological Seminary*

> "Can you imagine a daily visit with one of the saints gone by? Here's your chance. Bernard's book will take you back to the soul of some of Christendom's experts on the devotional life. If you need spiritual uplifting as much as I do, you'll thank the Lord for this book."—*Charlie Shedd, author of the multi-million sellers* Letters to Karen *and* Letters to Philip